Praise for *Reduced to Joy*

Reduced to Joy has many different kinds of poems, all of them clear, wise, beautifully put, spare. Mark Nepo has a great heart. His poems are good company.

—Coleman Barks,
translator of *The Essential Rumi*

Mark Nepo's poems in his new book, *Reduced to Joy*, reduce me first to grateful silence, and then to tears, and then to laughter, and then to praise. He joins a long tradition of truth-seeking, wild-hearted poets—Rumi, Walt Whitman, Emily Dickinson, Mary Oliver—and deserves a place in the center of the circle with them.

—Elizabeth Lesser, cofounder of the Omega Institute,
author of *Broken Open: How Difficult Times Can Help Us Grow*

Please, open this book. Begin anywhere. Take your time. But know this: Mark Nepo will make you fall in love with the world. Again.

—Wayne Muller,
author of *A Life of Being, Having and Doing Enough* and *Sabbath*

These poems touch the soul, reminding each of us what it means to be fully alive, to be surrounded by what is sacred. Allow them to reach under your skin, to where mystery is born into meaning.

—Llewellyn Vaughan-Lee, Ph.D.,
Sufi teacher and author of *Prayer of the Heart*

Oh! What a marvelous book. Mark Nepo's generous, vast poems restore readers to joy even before we finish reading them—musing upon single lines, images, stanzas—we feel it rising up again, that precious sense of YES. And completing them—we feel the rich trove of thinking and living so heartened and restored.

—Naomi Shihab Nye,
author of *Words Under the Words* and *19 Varieties of Gazelle*

Rumi would have described this book of poems as a crystal chandelier—so many jewels, each like a treasure God has placed in the heart of Mark Nepo. If you already know Mark's work, you won't want to miss this collection. And if you have never had the pleasure of experiencing the world through Mark Nepo's eyes, begin with *Reduced to Joy*.

—Gayatri Naraine,
coauthor of *Something Beyond Greatness*

By having, as he puts it, nothing to say, Mark Nepo says everything in this new book of poems. By showing us again and again what happens when one person "works toward peace," we witness what is possible when we are "reduced to joy" by an honest life, and by poetry itself.

—Phil Cousineau,
author of *The Art of Pilgrimage* and *The Painted Word*

Nepo's voice, clear, resonant, and real, acts like the pointer on your heart's compass and helps you navigate your most joyful life.

—Mary Anne Radmacher,
author of *Lean Forward into Your Life* and *She*

I am deeply moved by Mark Nepo's work, especially the healing power of the writing process he brings through to us all. His new *Reduced to Joy* cuts close to the bone with passages of pure beauty and raw honesty. I felt the stillness he wrote of, followed by a sense of peace. For this, I am grateful.

—Nina Lesowitz,
coauthor of *Living Life as a Thank You*

In *Reduced to Joy*, Mark Nepo has written a love letter that speaks directly to the heart of the reader. He writes from the wisdom of experience—of having journeyed through two cancers. He gets to the essence of happiness, touching readers with his poetic passages and personal *aha* moments. He reminds us that in stillness, in embracing the mystery of life, and in embodying our birthright as mighty expressions of love, we are reduced to joy.

—Susyn Reeve,
author of *The Inspired Life:
Unleashing Your Mind's Capacity for Joy*

Nepo makes simple, often overlooked things in life, meaningful—and the meaningful, but sometimes overly complex things, simple. This is a beautiful book of poems to deepen and nurture the soul with love and joy, even for those who have never read a poem in their life.

—Allen Klein,
author of *The Art of Living Joyfully*

In *Reduced to Joy*, Mark Nepo's powerful and poignant collection of life poems, we are reminded again of what it is to be truly alive. His poems inspire, connect, and encourage us to breathe in our own truth so that we can rediscover the peace and joy that is also present in each moment of our lives.

—Polly Campbell,
author of *Imperfect Spirituality:*
Extraordinary Enlightenment for Ordinary People

reduced
to joy

Also by Mark Nepo

reduced
to joy

Mark Nepo

Foreword by
Wayne Muller

Published in the United States by Viva Editions, an imprint of Cleis Press, Inc., 2246 Sixth Street, Berkeley, California 94710.

Printed in the United States.
Cover design: Frank Wiedemann
Cover photograph: iStockphoto
Text design: Frank Wiedemann
First Edition.
10 9 8 7 6 5 4 3 2 1

Trade paper ISBN: 978-1-936740-57-4
E-book ISBN: 978-1-936740-66-6

Library of Congress Cataloging-in-Publication Data

Nepo, Mark.
 Reduced to Joy : Poems / Mark Nepo. -- First Edition.
    pages cm
 ISBN 978-1-936740-57-4 (Trade Paperback) -- ISBN 978-1-936740-66-6 (E-book)
 I. Title.
 PS3564.E6R43 2013
 811'.54--dc23
                        2013020163

I want nothing more than to speak simply,
to be granted this grace.
For we have burdened even our song with so much music
that it is slowly sinking
and we have embellished our art so much that the goldwork
has eaten away its face
and it is time to say our few words because tomorrow
our soul sets sail.

—George Seferis

...for Susan
whose laugh is to joy
as birds are to light...

Contents

FOREWORD

Mark may be the most quietly honest poet of our generation. He tends so fiercely to the simple truth of being alive. Precise and tender, he shows us where to look till we remember things precious or lost, things we forgot we knew.

Many people find reassuring comfort in Mark's writing. His poetic prose touches our shared humanity in places intimate, painful, and beautiful. But I have for years watched people hear Mark's poetry for the first time. I tell you, they are changed. One poem is sufficient; the world is never the same.

Please, open this book. Begin anywhere. Take your time. But know this: Mark Nepo will make you fall in love with the world. Again.

—Wayne Muller, author of
A Life of Being, Having and Doing Enough
and *Sabbath*

About Joy

Often, what keeps us from joy is the menacing assumption that life is happening other than where we are. So we are always leaving, running from or running to. All the while, joy rises like summer wind, waiting for us to grow in the open, large as willows it can sing through. Yet failing to grow in the open, we can be worn to it. Though working with what we're given till it wears us through seems to be the grace we resist. Like everyone, I've spent so much of my life fearing pain that I've seldom felt things all the way through. And falling through more than working through, I've learned that if we can stay true to our experience and to each other, and face the spirit that experience and love carry, we will eventually be reduced to joy. Like cliffs worn to their beauty by the pounding of the sea, if we can hold each other up, all that will be left will be wonder and joy.

—MN

LEFT IN THE OPEN

The longest journey you will
make in your life
is from your head to your heart.

—an old Sioux saying

THREE FACES

I have carried three faces
across my life, though from within,
it's clear, they have carried me:

a woman who can stare through
the leaves of any tree, who names the
tree by the birds who sing in it

a man who works hard at
clearing paths in order to stop
where the path ends, and listen

and a small child with the heart
of a horse, eager to sniff out any
thing alive and run to it.

Together, they have led who I
thought I was through openings

wide enough for only
what is essential.

FEELING THE OAR

I was in the air, frustrated
that fog had delayed us. Now,
I would miss my flight to Dallas
where I was on my way to speak
about obstacles as teachers.

I was feeling pissed off
when I noticed my left hand
on the seat—it was my father's
hand—the large knuckles, the
pronounced veins, the bark-like
wrinkles at the base of my thumb.

It was his hand as I had seen it
countless times: guiding a piece of
wood through a band saw or tapping
on an open book as he would
try to understand.
I opened and closed it like

someone waking from a long sleep.

It is the hand I write with. And it
is weathered, an immigrant hand,
rough from crossing many seas.

Had it not been for the fog and the
delay, I wouldn't have noticed.

I touched it with my other hand;
trying to know my father,
trying to feel the oar,
trying to remember the sea.

Is There Any Other Question?

You ask, "Am I foolish to want her so badly?"
And I think of waiting in the rain to bump into
Susan on the corner of Robin and Myrtle. It was
a day that changed my life. I can still see her walking
back to work, my heart knowing in that moment—
I couldn't never-see-her-again. So you're
asking the wrong person. You lean forward,
rubbing the place she has broken, and say,
one more time, "I need to see if she's changed."

I only know that some are born to love one thing
and can't escape it any more than the bee can escape
the flower it is born to enter. Or the flower escape
being chewed by a starving deer. And some, having
been entered or chewed, are worn to love everything
the way silence soothes every cry. The way water softens
every bit of life that falls into it. Do we take turns?
Is that it? Loving one thing, then everything?

I see your pain noosed by your hope. Oh if I could
keep you from your dream of being held and her
fear of being known, I'd turn you into a hawk in
glide who asks nothing of the sky. Only humans
suffer loss, drop their heads, and carve out why.
Have we loved well? Can anyone tell?

No, not a hawk, but a whale who mates for life,
who sings and circles unknown reefs, taking
mystery like water in through its teeth.

There have been times I've been hurtful or
forgotten who you are, times I've mistaken
you for one of the dark faces I've never put to
rest. Times you've done the same. Times we've
worked out our pain or fear, using each other
as the block of wood to carve our way to truth;
feeling awful when we remember that the one
we carve is the one who has loved us through
everything.

But this is the messy art of facing things:
knocking over what I love with what
I avoid; only to learn again that
this is not of our timing.

It doesn't matter what thorns we carry
or how we squirm to avoid their pain.
We unfold as long as we love,
pried into blossom.

My love for you has outlasted my notions
of love, the way a redwood, allowed to stand
after many storms, grows from the inside,
forcing its bark to drop away.

My friend has died and the grass is
growing as I watch the logs dry and
crack in the garage. Yesterday, I saw a
lone worm leave the heartwood as if
waiting till it was safe. I wonder what
lone secret left Steve's heart after he
died before the medics arrived. Is it
hiding in his closet or in our grief?
Is this the relentless, resilient way,
that what survives moves from one
carrier to the next? There are buds
on the maple though it is October.
Even wet concrete seems beautiful.
If I knew the question, I'd ask it
of everyone.

Coming Out

While there is much to do
we are not here to do.

Under the want to problem-solve
is the need to being-solve.

Often, with full being
the problem goes away.

The seed being-solves its
darkness by blossoming.

The heart being-solves its loneliness
by loving whatever it meets.

The tea being-solves the water
by becoming tea.

When I looked in your eye, the light was just right.
I could make out the markings behind your seeing,
through which you perceive everything. There was the
door you hid behind as a child, the wood through which
your father's voice would raise. And the neighbor's bird
feeder which you could see from your first apartment,
the one the goldfinch would dart in, that spring we
fell in love. And the photo of your Uncle Billy standing
with a mug of coffee, listening softly to everything you
ever wanted to say. Sometimes, when alone enough,
before you're up, I stare into the mirror in the guest
room, reaching for the markings behind my eye. This
is harder but they are there. How I would wheeze as a
boy in the dark wondering about God. My first glimpse
of the Pacific after college. And Grandma's thick open
palms that fed goats in Russia, that felt the ocean through
the hull of the ship that brought her to America, the hands
that rubbed her chest when her Nehemiah died. It's hard to
say how, but I see life through the water of her palms. How

does this work? How does the heart like the bottom of a river
keep shifting its features? To graduate into the world, we are
required to memorize practical and odd things: the number
of feet in a mile, the year Henry VIII beheaded Anne Boleyn,
the degree at which clouds will freeze their rain. But since
death is the mirror we eventually move through, let's stop
carrying the things we repeat and start holding things
with our eyes. To know by heart is to warm the
broken as they lay down in the sand of our eyes.

Standing in the harbor, these slick
wonders slip their fins in and out
of early sun. I close my eyes and remember being wheeled into surgery
all those years ago; believing my job
was to meet my surgeon at the surface, so the rib he had to remove
would slip out, like a dolphin of
bone, as soon as he would cut me.

I've learned that everything that
matters goes the way of the dolphin:
drifting most of the time out of
view, breaking surface when
we least expect it.

And our job—in finding God, in
being God; in finding truth, in
being truth; in finding love, in

being love—is to meet the world
at the surface where Spirit slips
out through every cut.

ONE STRING

I am so busy at times
trying to make it all
worthwhile, that I am
stunned at how easily the
whole of life speaks to me,
when music I've never heard
or a truth I never understood
plucks the one string I carry
deep within.

I only want that string pluck-
ed and yet, it stays in a place
only suffering or surrender
can open.

Still, violins in minor keys
make me swallow my fear
and herons flying into
the end of a long day

make me wish I'd led

a more peaceful life.

I'm saved by what is timeless.
Can taste it though it fills no cup.
Can feel it though it can't be seen.

Yesterday, an old brooding song was
sung low, making the afternoon drop
its shoulders. Even the wind circled
back. I dropped my napkin, glad to
feel that old ache waiting like a lucky
coin I rub but seldom look at. Everyone broods and holds on to what they
think is lucky.

I'm saved by your laugh, which stops the
crows of pleasure and pain from pecking
at each other inside my head.

This morning I tried three times to read
something I've wanted to read for years.

But you were sick and the car broke
down. And waiting for the tow truck,
I stood in the shade of a locust tree.
The patches of sun reminded me
that we've already arrived.

On the Way to Windsor

By what road did you come?
I can tell by your eyes—
you lost something along the way.
Were you hurt or did you do the hurting?
Me? Both.

Did you drop anything willingly?
I know. That's a hard one.
I seem to have lost everything
that identifies me.
My heart's become a knapsack
with torn little holes.
I knew we'd meet like this.

Oh, there are those who keep to themselves.
When the wind sounds like a loved one,
they come out and squint.
But tell me, what does it mean
to dream on this side of suffering?

That we can rest more?
That we can hear small birds
unlace the dawn?

It seems very simple now.
We can finally talk when there isn't
much to say. It's quite beautiful,
isn't it?

UNDER BIRDSONG

Over half a century of staying awake,
or trying, and what do I know, really?
That after falling, the sky seems brighter?
That after listening, love seems possible?
That after succumbing to silence, the
lone root inching under everything
needs to be held too?

All this and a thousand implications
surface as "I love you" or "I am afraid."

We are just lone birds flushed out of
hiding, surprised so small a throat
can cough up a song.

As soon as I could walk, I was told of death
by those afraid of time. Others have warned
me of life. And some have said, forget all that,
we are here to live. A few have thrown them
all in the sky like wet stars, saying, in time
you will see the constellation they form.

It was an old woman losing her way
who called me close. She tapped my chest
with her crooked finger and said, stay
ultimately concerned, about everything.

In getting there, I've seen how life is
layered from the outside and vital from
within; beautifully designed to strip us
of our burden—if we can drop through
the layers or ride what is vital.

But here you are, and seeing you rub

your eyes as you shuffle in the light, I'm
bursting to offer a hand, to say something
helpful. Though as I reach for you, *I*
trip and, taking *your* hand, forget
what it might be.

BEHIND THE THUNDER

People say we're all seeking a meaning for life. I don't think that's what we're really seeking. I believe we're seeking an experience of being alive.

—Joseph Campbell

So Much Is Carried
(for Saba)

When just a pup, I took her into winter.
While Paul photographed the heavy snow,
she, having never run free, circled wildly,
her little nose caked with white.

She slipped and broke the ice. I can still
see her puppy face underwater, looking
for a way out, her tiny paws swatting
at the thick clear deep.

With no thought, I was waist high and
wet, sweeping her into the air. She flew
a good twelve feet and landed with a thud.
She shook and started to shiver. We rubbed
her down for two hours, blowing her with
an old hair dryer. I held her in my shirt,
near my heart, the whole way home.

I'm fourteen years and seven states away
and she has died. My first dog. I close
my eyes and there she is, grown,
sniffing the air in an open field,
smelling things I couldn't even sense.

How many times I've played that day
in the pond: her struggle underwater,
her drying on my chest.

How much that day has shaped my art:
always jumping in and sweeping what
has been baptized in the deep back
into the world, always holding it
near my heart. As if my life
depends on it.

I can still taste lying with you
in the afternoon during the storm,
lost in your eyes. After all we know
about each other, I'm stopped by how
our fingers Braille each other's face.

A few days ago, I held a friend
as he cried, could feel his pain
in my chest.

Some thirty years ago, I held my
brother when his best friend died
from spinal meningitis. I don't think
he's ever been the same. And last night
I dreamt about the death of my parents;
my father longing to hold me, my
mother turning away. None of us
able to find each other.

I don't know where this is going.
None of us do. But I wake sometimes
like a humble gardener on a ladder, who
keeps discovering that the edge of the garden
is farther than he'd imagined. I wake with
this bag of red seed, each filled with light
from the beginning, and I keep spilling
them like tears.

I woke today with a sadness.
I don't know why. Perhaps one
of the lost crossed the morning sun
like a crow, just long enough to cast
a small shadow on my heart.

Now I feel hungry.
Sometimes we eat not to feel
our sadness. And not just food.
We eat books with our eyes, the
past with our memories, and
uncertainty with our schemes.

Sometimes, we make maps
and eat them, all to avoid
the fact that we will always
run out of time.

People I have loved have gone

missing or turned away. Some
in their sadness tried to eat me.
And so, I had to leave.

Perhaps that's it. Though
we have to leave or be left,
The heart never leaves. And
standing in that shadow,
We feel sad.

Everyone keeps stopping me with their urgency.
As if the secret of life was written in a corner
of their mind and before they could
read it, it burst aflame.

The first hundred times, I rushed to do their
bidding. Then one day, exhausted by my own
secrets burning, I stopped running and
kissed everything on fire.

And yes, it scarred my lip and now
I have trouble saying anything complicated,
but wind no longer gets trapped in my head.

I know you understand. I've seen you suffer
the secrets no one asked us to keep secret. I've
seen them burning up your mind. But today,
we can part the veils and let in whatever
it is we thought we had to keep out.

Today, urgency dies because the heart
has burned its excuses.

I'm in the Sacramento zoo where they
specialize in vanishing animals. I'm staring
into a dusty yard where a Bongo from Africa
is sleeping in the heat, his dark mask and
white horns like a Picasso come to life.

He knows the world by his huge ears and
wet nose. He dreams of yams and cassavas.
He's looking at me. Intensely at first, but he
can tell I'm no threat. He relaxes and simply
stares like a sage from another world. He's
searching my face as he would a cave
for markings from long ago.

He seems to be reading what I've
carried but can't decipher. His stare says,
Not much difference to which side of the fence
we look out from, is there? I wish I could

understand Bongo. He's done with
me and looks away.

Now that my father can
barely walk, I send him
socks to keep him warm.
He's overjoyed. Now that
he can't go very far, he finally
has time to wonder what I do.
Now he travels backwards and
tells me of his first chisels,
his love of wood. We have
small conversations that rise
like smoke from the fire in
the mountain of fathers and
sons. After years of silence,
it's more than enough.

I keep looking for one more teacher,
only to find that fish learn from water
and birds learn from sky.

If you want to learn about the sea,
it helps to be at sea.
If you want to learn about compassion,
it helps to be in love.
If you want to learn about healing,
it helps to know of suffering.

The strong live in the storm
without worshipping the storm.

On Every Corner
(for Saki & Rachmana)

Sunday morning, the table scattered with
bagels, toast, ham and tea, breaded knives on
crumpled napkins, books on every corner—
Whitman, Doty, Jacques Prevert, Rumi on
the floor—each of us tossing another voice
into the air to see what's folded way inside,
to see what lives between yesterday and the
sugar. Each of us knowing what it's like to be
both turtle and hawk, and Hamlet, all in a day.
The dog sleeps on Kenyon, near Neruda, as we
reach for something not quite in reach and
land on each other, as if the one utterance
inside every voice can soften the onslaught
of time.

For the Moment

It was in Vancouver
at breakfast, before my
second cup of coffee.
I had a moment, a long
moment, before the next
task showed its teeth,
before the meetings began,
and the clink of silverware
glistened slightly, and the
coffee warmed my throat,
and I fell into the well of
a silence that was there
before I was born.

For the moment, the
thing that waits behind
my tongue dropped way
down behind my heart,
like an iridescent fish

hovering under all that
water near the center
of the Earth.

Now the phone is
ringing. The emails are
flitting, and the voices
in the hive of which I
am a part are mounting.

But the coffee is
steaming and my mind
for now is clear and the
path between it and my
heart is open and I
finally have nothing
to say.

MADE FROM BONE

When I can be the truth,
it grows more and more clear
when it is necessary to tell the truth.

That is, when I have access to the place
within me that is lighted, I don't have
to speak heatedly. I can just give away
warmth. When I am still enough to brush
quietly with eternity, I don't have to
speak of God. I can just offer peace
to those around me.

A tree grows so it can convey wind.
It is not the wind. And a person grows
in order to convey spirit.

They say that animals recharge
their innocence each time they hoof
the earth. And we are reborn

each time we touch what matters.

As the wind makes a different song
through the same tree as its branches
break, God makes finer and finer music
through the wearing down of our will.

We loved so blindly,
each one of us meaning
to explore the other's face

but knocking over
everything
in the way.

Now, we build
dark images of
what we think happened.

I heard a song today
that played when we
were young.

It made me ache
to have you all near

just for a long minute
in which none of us
could speak.

FOR JOEL AT 94

They say that miners in South America
strap small lamps around their chest, that
this works better than the light coming
from the center of your head.

They say the head can be fooled,
but the heart can't turn without
the body. This makes me think of you
digging your way through your long life,
lighting everything with your heart.

It's a good way to live. And when we
sit at the end of the day, our hearts
illumine the day and we see each other
in its radiance. I can tell, it reminds you
of many circles you've been a part of.
It's a good way to measure time.

To make our way on Earth

by the light coming from our heart—
This is what you've taught us.

Is it any wonder that what you
touch, including us, glows.

A small blurry figure appears at the
doorway of the home. It is Bella, my
Russian Jewess, on a ramp in a wheel-
chair, waving her stick at me; a first
born of a first born of a first born.
She is beckoning, "Here. For you.
A lollipop." I am 3. She, 105.
Darkly dressed relatives line the
ramp like pines waiting for wind.

She gloats on her spoked throne.
I'm her immigrant heir. The pines
rustle. Her bony hands are cold. She
grips me above my elbows.

She mouths something in a language
I don't understand. The pines approve.
Her stick slips to the ramp. She runs

her fingers behind my ears. Her stiff
thumbs rub my temples.

She pulls me to her and the cold
footplates crease my ankles. She
whispers something in my ear.
Her breath is short and stale.

She picks up her stick and presses
it to my palm like a scepter. I give it
back. The tall pines sigh. She looks
skyward and rocks. I feel her breath
even now, fifty years on.

This is my first memory
and I wonder what she carried
from the beginning and where the
things that matter that we don't
understand live.

Sometimes, when whispering in
snow to no one, I wonder if

the long search for poetry
has all been to find
what she said to me.

TILL WE KNOW
EACH OTHER

And what if we're meant to discover
that caring for another is the summit?

He was born in the river of yes
but looking for love wandered into
the industry of no, where the no-police
left warnings of don't and the no-ministers
preached their morals of can't. And soon,
he couldn't help himself, he wanted to
try on no. So when his dog pawed his
shirt, he scolded her no, and when
two kids ran a shopping cart into his
parked car, he cuffed them no. And
when someone he liked started to come
close, he let her near but said he wasn't
ready. Now he discovered there were
other ways to say no. When he was hired
as a no-engineer, he was sadly happy to work
alone. Steadily, he designed signs that said
stop and electronic guns that fired bullets
with a muffled no. The work of no kept
him very busy. If you called, you heard, "I

am the engineer of no and I am not here.
If you like, leave a no-message and I will
gladly send a no-reply." He was flooded with
calls. The industry of no was so successful, it
had to hide its money from the government,
lest they say no. When he was promoted to
find other avenues of no, he rode no-planes
to no-cafes where inventors of no pleaded
for new no-funding. Soon, there were movies
that glorified no, and books that pondered
why the no-God was so insistent on no. And
seminars arose where no-scholars came vast
distances to say, "Yes, it has always been a
world of no." And those specially invited
stroked their worried chins, whispering
to each other, "It is so. It is so," as a no-
anthropologist traced the beginnings
of no. But they all went home and
dreamt of white geese flapping,
their wings parting
the ancient air.

On her porch, on the mesa, we're sipping
tea, when Julie begins to speak of storms and
how the birds she feeds perch on her roof and
answer the thunder. Wayne sees how this hits me,
knows at once I will enter this poem. Because this
is the nature of all poems. This is what we long
for: to cry out with our little thunder to the big
thunder. To ask in our small way: how to love the
storm without getting struck. I wonder what the
thunder and birds talk about. I look at my friends
and confess that what I know has been split like a tree
by lightning. Julie's dogs take off, chasing something
we can't hear. And the birds circle as if to say, keep
talking. We move on to failed relationships and
pottery. Wayne slouches. I can see his heart peck
like a bird behind his eyes. Julie says that African
potters spend long days coiling their pots and when
they're done, when the thing they've built around
the empty center is fired, they uncoil the air the

same number of times to free the spirit of the pot.
Westerners think it superstitious, but the old potters
believe it necessary to uncoil themselves like spirits
trapped in pots. Wayne nods. He feels all coiled
and says, "The heart grows tired of its reasons."
After a long silence, the dogs lie down, the birds
vanish, the clouds travel to tempt others, and
we are left to face each other; unfiltered
through what we want or love.

The bees are penetrating the small blue flowers.
The fiddler with dirty teeth just broke a string
but his banjo man keeps playing. The young
university girls are picking at their salads. In a
counter window, a squid is puckering in a tub of
ice while the Hispanic girl working there is leaning
on the tub reading a book. The Copper River salmon,
though dead on ice, are dreaming of their last turn
upstream. The ferns on the rooftop are feathered in
the salty wind. People crisscross the cobblestone
with their history and dreams in tow like cells in
the immune system looking for dark places to heal.
The mountains, snow covered across the bay,
resist it all. A young Asian couple ask a Black
woman to take their picture before the sea.
At the last second, a gull cuts through
the frame. They won't notice till
they are far away at home.

How Spirit Works on Earth

I hiked the low mountains with a friend and
we stumbled on a snake, as frightened as I.
Somehow that led my friend to speak of her
father, ninety and going blind. After a day
of stumbles, of getting lost and falling
down, he said, his flint all chipped,
"I've learned how to love what is."

The next day I felt lonely and settled
in the corner of a Spanish café where I
overheard a young widow miss her man.
Her friend kept rubbing her arm. After three
lattes, the widow dried her eyes with a brown
napkin and admitted that she kept meeting a
stray collie in the cemetery. She wasn't sure,
but took the dog home. She swears her
man sent the dog to comfort her.

I called Paul and asked what he thought.

He sighed and told me how years ago, in
another life, a man appeared at his door
and said, "I lived in this house as a boy."
The guy seemed strange. He asked to come
in, then looked about and nodded to himself,
"I'd like to plant some wildflowers out back."
Paul hesitated, then agreed. They developed
an odd friendship. Paul learned that Will
was a janitor who played in a symphony,
who loved Handel and haiku, and read
a lot about alchemy. When the wildflowers took root, Will vanished.

Paul shrugged, "You ask about Spirit?
I often think, I could have been Will. Or
the widow's collie. Or the curb the old man
tripped on." That night I dreamt that Will
and the collie were shuffling through a field
alight in sudden sun. Will kept tossing a stick—
it seemed golden in the air—and the collie kept
bringing it back. When I caught up with them,
the collie dropped the stick like a treasure at

my feet. Will smiled, "It all goes out and
comes back. Like this stick. That's how it
works." Before I could ask, Will threw
the stick further. The collie chased it.
And I woke back in my loneliness.

Now you call to tell me of a plaza in
Nicaragua where street musicians play
and the parrots sing along. But when the
musicians stop, the birds don't come. This
is why you called. You are concerned and
in wonder. I love you for calling. I love
you for being so concerned. You are
stunned by this law of spirit, "When
we stop singing in the open, the birds
don't come." We both go silent. I close
my eyes, wishing you were here.

On certain Sundays in the late fifties,
my father's four uncles would sweep into
our home like a tornado of laughter and
take us to the local pool hall. They were
weathered immigrants from Russia—Max,
Al, Norton, and Axi. They'd sharked their
way through the Depression, running the
table, throwing money in a jar. Once Axi,
hit by a car, broke his thumb, but cursed,
played and won, before having it set. That's
how he got his name: Axi, for accident. My
father always opened up a little more around
them. I used to wake on Sundays and hope,
the way quiet children pray in secret for
gypsies to arrive. But what I remember
most is being knee-high, not quite able to
see the table, their laughter circling like the
gods of Olympus tossing their losses into the
sea. My brother and I would run through their

legs. We couldn't make out all that was said.
But the smell of chalk, and swift strokes scat-
tering bright balls, the thunder of resilience
that parted life's harshness—it made me feel
happy and safe. Sometimes I'd grab one of their
legs like the tree of life itself. Now, when beat
up and sad, I find myself drifting into some
bar, looking for a cue. Then I take the years
off like a coat, chalk up and sigh; leaning
over the felt table, waiting for their
laughter to swallow the world.

He couldn't find a place to tie his camel
when a quiet man in a uniform took the reins
and showed him inside. He sat for the longest
time on a sofa staring at the enormous chandelier. So many jewels, he thought, each like a soul
God has placed on Earth and scattered. He felt
the chandelier was a messenger, saying without
saying, "When you can come together like this,
your love will conquer gravity and you will hover
like this enormous, glittering light." Just then, a
pretty young woman asked if he wanted to register.
He wasn't sure what that meant but he went along.
In the days that followed, he kept seeing the many
jewels scattered. Then others came and brought
him to meetings where he listened to men and
women carve up the resources of their great nation.
And beneath the noise of their benevolence, he
could see inside their chests, where each carried
a light that was throbbing below their proposals.

When it was his turn, he whirled around the room, touching each jewel's heart. Then he sat and stared at his hand. Finally, the leader of the group leaned over and gently asked, "What does this mean?" Instead of talking, he took the leader's hand and put it on his heart. Well, the meeting was no longer a meeting, and some wanted to get closer, while others wanted to run. He was driven back to the hotel where he spent the afternoon listening to the chandelier.

It could be the letter never answered,
the one in which you declared your love
in such a tender way, admitting to everything. Or when the shell you brought all
the way from the Philippines is dropped
by some loud stranger you never wanted
to show it to in the first place. It could all
unravel the moment the shell shatters on
your floor. Or on a summer bench, your
eyes closed, your fear about to vanish, the
heat bathing you as bees begin to fly.

It could happen anywhere you linger
too long, anywhere you stop hauling and
counting, when your mind spills its tangle
of lists. Often it comes with the relaxation
of great pain. When the hip finally mends
enough to step. Or your need to know
is broken by a bird lifting into light.

Or when succeeding in being something you're not. Being influential when you're shy. Or rugged when you're tender.

Or while watching an old tree slip into winter, like the one thing you won't let go of dropping all its leaves.

When the elements in all their beauty reshape our eyes, it is God's kiss: gentle as erosion. When you could crumble in an instant—all your pain, salt waiting for a wave—you are close.

—*Forgive me.*
I loved a woman who loved the Earth.

I met a man who was going there,
where you had lifted the faces of children.
He works where you are buried. He
scratched his chin and said, "I know
someone is out there, beneath a tree,
but I don't know who she was."

When you were dying, your thin
wrist in my hand, I knew I'd be here,
in this day, busting with my sense of
you before people who never
heard your voice.

Forgive me. It's impossible
to keep your memory alive.
Even your father never sent me

the picture that split me with an ache,
the one with long brown hair
from years before we met.

He never sent it, though I asked
three times. And now like all memorials,
the spirit's gone, aerating the earth
and stone is stone, tree is tree
except your ash has fed its root.

Forgive me. I keep writing your name
but can't out-write the wave of life
that sweeps you from the sand.

No matter how I sing of you,
there's always someone who appears
just as I'm finished. I can't keep up.

Even when I stand before strangers
and say, I loved her so, my words rise
in the air above their hearts
and I can't stay the silence,

the merciless patient silence
which waits for every cry to fade
into that sea of God
that frees us
of our names.

WITHOUT KNOWING

Lifting my second coffee to my lips,
I see a young couple near the window.
They're falling in love. I can tell by the
way he brushes her hair aside, so he can
see her face. Before I can sip, there you
are, across from me, more than forty
years ago. I did the same thing. Parting
your auburn hair, I fell into your eyes.
It undid me, which meant I could no
longer follow the path others had set
for me. Isn't this the purpose of love?
We only had a few years of opening
what we could in each other, before
you fell into another. You broke my
heart. It took a decade of poking at the
ashes to accept that we sent each other
on our way. Now, in my sixties, after
losing and finding what matters, enough
times to realize that the losing and find-

ing comes and goes like surf that shapes
the sand of our heart, I know I fell *through*
your eyes, so many years ago, into the sweet,
resilient place only opened by love, where
we get to see our own worth, unformed
like raw material. It takes years of ham-
mering and being hammered to see
what we can shape from what we're
given. Strange to pick up this conversation now. I take another sip, and
through the steam, can see the young
woman glimpse her worth briefly in her
jittery, young man. I sip and feel the gift
you were without your even knowing. I
don't even know if you're still alive. But
in this café, from another continent
of time, I can softly thank you.

WHAT OTHERS HAVE TOUCHED

When his grandson was born, he
began collecting antique toys—a torn
doll, a wooden rabbit, a cloth bear.
He loves to see his little one touch
what others have touched.

When told it had to go, she refused
to cut the old apple tree, though its roots
are buckling the driveway. She doesn't need
the apples. It's the deer. Every fall she shakes
the upper branches from a ladder. She loves
the small thuds to the ground. She loves
early coffee as they soft-hoof and nibble.

When Jess and Laura were small, I
bought earrings in Florence. I'm saving
them till they turn sixteen. I love thinking of the earrings waiting in my closet
for them to grow.

When in Amsterdam, he thought
the museums would grab him, but it
was a sloppy Newfoundland wading
in a reflecting pool; splashing patches
of water filled with sun, then trying
to bite the splashes. He loves to think
of the soul's journey this way.

When Grandma made potato pancakes
on her small stove, it smelled like burnt
French toast. I'd sit on a stool in the corner
and she'd mat one on some napkins, blow
on it, and give it to me. She's been gone
twenty years. But I love how she
cooks them for me in my dreams.

WE'VE COME TO THIS

We've known each other for 26 years,
across 18 states, through storms
we feared would never let up.

We held each other when marriages
failed, through accidents and cancers.
We held each other up when
our grandmothers died.

I've seen you in the rain
where words can't reach you.
I've even seen the rain
that is yours alone.

And here, now, as if life has been
a climb to this view—the privilege of
asking again, as if for the first time,
who are you?

We've endured cold mothers
and absent fathers and the breakage
of belief which, snapped like a pole,
brought down our tents.

But here we are.

I look at you, after all these years,
without protection, and say,
I want to know you.

Whatever you've withheld,
whatever I've not been able to
hear, let's sit in the clearing
and understand each other
like old birds whose wings
are used now
more to huddle
than to fly.

How hard it is to leave or be
left. Sending someone away
because violence is near. Or
selling all you have so a child
might have a ticket to a better
life. Or those torn from each
other because the ship could
hold no more. Or inexplicably
when the love is gone. Or some
strange need has awakened after
years and one of you must try
again to be what you failed to be.

Yet what if, when all alone, we
open a letter, addressed to who
we are under everything, that says:
beyond our pain, each gasp of
parting pollinates the world with
what the heart releases when it

feels the most. This sharp honey
keeps the world from falling.

It doesn't make it easier. I
still can't bear to think of
losing you. But nor can the
clouds bear to lose their rain.

An old president died just hours after a young
man from Idaho was shot in his sleep in Iraq, and
now in the Sundarban east of the Himalayas, a tiger
licks the eyes of its newborn yet to see, and further east
in Vietnam, a young woman who has worked very hard
to learn how to read is reciting a sutra from Buddha,
in awe how presence moves through words across
the centuries. At the same time, an unwed mother
in Chicago thinks about stealing a blanket as
winter stiffens, and moments after this, a
manta ray in Ecuador wakes because of the
sun's heat on its back and its sweep over coral
startles the moray back into its nook, and as the
old president's body cools, a sergeant finds the
boy from Idaho. And just now, in Chile, a
tired couple re-see each other and make love
in the afternoon while clouds come in from the
Pacific. And just now, you stir, the dog stretches,
and far away, two stars collide, a new world forms,

and somewhere between the city and the sea, a child
is born with an untempered capacity to love. In time,
he or she will want to love us all. Remember their
face, though you have never seen it. Speak their
name, though you have never heard it. Mistake
everyone for them. Love everything in the way.

What if I'm the son of a 92-year-old man
who can hardly walk from the kitchen to
the couch in the home where I grew up,
which is flooded by a storm whose wet arms
covered a thousand miles. What if I can't
reach him because the phone he can't find
is wet and has no power. What if a month
later I travel to Cambodia on a trip that took
five years to save for, and out of breath I stare
for an hour at a thousand-year-old face carved
at Angkor Wat. What if that eyeless face makes
me question what I've done with my life. What
if I can't stop thinking of my father struggling
to pick up a spoon. What if on the plane home
the woman next to me dreams of her mother's
mother picking lemons in Sicily. What if the
thousand angels, who never rest, work in each
of us, the way immune cells rush to the site of
a wound. What if all this keeps me from sleep-

ing. What if I fear that I will never sleep again.
What if, as the plane slips through the throat
of dawn, it comes to me that we're not supposed to find something new all the time,
but weave each truth we find into a strong,
beautiful rope that the next generation can
climb. What if I admit that I found nothing
to bring home to my father, except the heart
of a son carved out by time. What if everything
we do and everywhere we go is for this end.
What if the heart carved out is what
can shelter us from the storm.

FROM NOW TO NOW

To be poured into without becoming full
and to pour out without becoming empty,
without knowing how this is brought about...

—Chuang-Tzu

I return by plane to read some poems.
There's Linanne and Nancy, widows of
friends I tell strangers I knew—how John
liked shrimp and night skies, how Wally
would laugh while crushing his cigarettes.

There's Father Malecki who dragged me
onto his raft of love when I was drowning
in cancer. And my former wife Ann—how
we struggled like fish flopping in the rapids.
And two students mature as oak, decades
into their lives; their reluctant husbands
dragged to see some relic from their past.

It all settles in this dizzy, small moment
I sometimes dream of but never expect.
Like those rare times as a boy when I'd
leap off the ground and throw the ball
cleanly through the net.

In this winded moment, we seem so
present that we rise above our wounds
and something drops through the net
of my heart, leaving me perfectly
empty and utterly complete.

Sometimes, our dog gets that look in her eye and
starts running full speed in circles and crazy-eights,
leaping over flowers and through the aging trees.

Sometimes, before I leave, Susan is under the covers,
her cheek showing, our dog curled in the crook of her
legs as close as she can get. I behold them, in the
dark, wondering how anything could be so at rest.

Sometimes, in their sleep, our dog twitches with
dreams of running and Susan smiles, as she
dreams of her garden growing.

As for me, I often do my best thinking as
the sun rises, like a giant eye brought alive
again by its first seeing.

What super-powers we've been given—
to ripple in motion and know the inside of air;

to stand in the dark and watch what we love;
to sleep with animals and simply dream; and
to see for the first time, more than once.

Sometimes, what seems ordinary exposes
its numinous bone, the way a man worn to love
can grow in the dark, just by aching for words.

When willful, we think
that truth moves from
our head to our heart
to our hands.

But bent by life,
it becomes clear that
love moves the other way:
from our hands to our
heart to our head.

Ask the burn survivor
with no hands who dreams
of chopping peppers and
onions on a spring day.

Or the eighty-year-old jazz
man who loses his hands
in a fog. He can feel them

but no longer entice them
to their magic.

Or the thousand-year-old
Buddha with no arms
whose empty eyes will
not stop bowing to the
unseeable center.

Truth flows from us,
or so we think, only
to be thrown back
as a surf of love.

Ask the aging painter
with a brush taped to his
crippled hand—wanting,
needing to praise it all
one more time.

After all this way,
I only want your questions.
The things you and I conclude
don't matter much.
I don't know why.
It just is so.

For all our talk of truth and God
won't insure that you and I
are true or holy.

Just feed me your questions.
I need them to keep this
fire going.

BIRDS IN AIR,
FISH IN WATER

A fish cannot drown in water.
A bird does not fall in air.
Each creature God made
must live in its own true nature.

—Mechthild of Magdeburg

After

After the Iliad, the Odyssey,
after the break, the being broken,
after the bondage, the wandering in the desert,
after the softening loss, the trail back to the beginning,
after the inner Iliad, the inner Odyssey,
after the clouding, the clearing,
after the clearing, another clouding,
after the dark tumble, the light,
after the light, another darkness,
after the blindness, another blindness,
after holding on, the sweet letting go,
after narrowing, the fall,
after sinking, the rising,
after rising, another sinking,
after falling in, the surprise
after everything, nothing,
after nothing, everything,
after the crucible that is you,
the world.

On the Ridge

We can grow by simply listening, the way the tree on
that ridge listens its branches
to the sky, the way blood
listens its flow to the site
of a wound, the way you
listen like a basin when
my head so full of grief
can't look you in the eye.
We can listen our way out
of anger, if we let the heart
soften the wolf we keep inside. We can last by listening
deeply, the way roots reach for
the next inch of earth, the way
an old turtle listens all he hears
into the pattern of his shell.

There have been many misunderstandings
along the way. But all can be forgiven
except the want to have us suppress
who we are: to make nice, to go
along, to defer our song.

And though elephants trudge miles
by the scent of their mammoth
hearts to honor one of their kind,
no tree fells itself so another can rise.

All to say that we are hunters
and gatherers inside as well:
striking down the other for food
or planting each other so we can
eat from how we grow.

ANIMAL BEING

Because we dream and want and carry on,
we think we're exempt. We think we're
above working the Earth on all fours.

We often miss the point.
A bear may feel like a hummingbird
the moment he catches a salmon,
but his paws are still paws.

As for me, I feel like a horse chasing
birds that cross the sky. When they fly
out of view, I know I'm a hawk born as
a horse. All poets are. A tangle of wings
and hooves. Trying to run in the sky
and fly on Earth.

So it's useless to pine for your lover
to be delicate, if she's really a cheetah.
Or for your mother to see clearly,

if her path is that of a bat.

It doesn't mean we can't try.
Just that we work
with what we're given.

THE THING ABOUT FEAR

We try to avoid it, distract ourselves,
even put others in the way. Because it
makes what is necessary seem monumental.
It makes what is needed seem uncrossable.
Yet when we stumble over the line, or are
loved over the line, or, in our exhaustion,
fall beyond our pain, what we feared
was a fall to our death turns out
to have been the next step.

AHYO-OH'-OH-NI

—from the Diné, to bring one
into harmony with everything.

When I open my tiny self,
I can almost hear the wood
growing inside the tree
and the love growing
inside your heart.

I can't hear it for long,
for my own creaking
takes over.

But there is this rhythm
of how things grow that
we are privy to from
time to time.

Don't give up

because your pain
sometimes drowns
out the Source.

FOR NINE-WEEK-OLD MIRA
TOO EXCITED TO SLEEP

I know, I know. There's bacon in the sink
and my slipper to shred. And that Shepherd
smell three houses down. But sleep, my puppy.
There will be other leaves to chase and sticks
to chew. You miss nothing when you sleep
but what it is to see you sleep: your lashes
twitting, your small eyes in dream, your
doggish yips, your belly in and out.

We watch you: pure eyes, pure run,
pure lick. Always needing to have
some part touch. Sleep, sweet puppy.
When you sleep, you stall us
into a softness we forget.

DISCERNMENT

The trouble with the mind
is that it sees like a bird
but walks like a man.

And things at the surface
move fast, needing to be
gathered. While things
at center move slow,
needing to be
perceived.

What I mean is
if you want to see the
many birds, you can
gather them in a cage
and wonder why
they won't fly.

Or you can go to

the wetlands, birding
in silence before
the sun comes up.

It's the same
with the things
we love or think.

We can frame them
in pretty cages or follow
them into the wild meadow
till they stun us with the
spread of their magnificent
wings.

QUIET, QUIET,
THE SMALL CREATURES
ARE TALKING

It was calculated that if you yell
for 8 years, 7 months and 6 days,
you will generate enough energy
to heat a cup of coffee.

Yet an ostrich has an eye bigger
than its brain and starfish have no
brains at all and the silky butterflies
taste with their feet.

So we have these choices: We can
yell and heat up. Or be still till our
eye perceives more than our brain.
Or spread like a star and give over
to the deep. Or open our pain till
we discover that the inside of the
heart is a kind of butterfly.
Then, we too can

taste with our feet.

To still all thought into a
seeing, to be carried by the
deep, to taste with our feet—
these are fates the saints
of all traditions fell into.

In here, the tongue is our
strongest muscle and
compassion
is its yoga.

Sometimes I move so fast it hurts.
Though the things coming at me
are not moving at all.

They are soft and inviting. It's
approaching them as if they will
vanish that makes them sharp.

Running into any point
makes it a knife.

ANOTHER PATIENCE

I wonder if flowers know fear,
if they sense a storm is coming
or if the deer will eat them? Or
if like a sage having exhausted
his humanity, the flower knows
that either way, broken or eaten,
the glow released is the same.
But I'm not a sage or a flower.
Teach me.

Till We Know Each Other

Butchers will tell you, if you don't
calm animals before slaughter,
the meat will be tough.

Yet zookeepers speak of the weight
of captivity: how if the beast gives in,
they're done; not worth showing
and not strong enough to set free.

Calm or tough, obedient or free,
it seems a mess: as if life throws us into
each other; one long outbreak of small
beings crying for power
because we feel so powerless.

So much depends on the drumming of soul
that opens the heart, the quieting of mind
that opens the eye, the acceptance of
others that softens the truth.

No one wants to admit
it is our suffering that awakens us
to the many ways we hold the gun.
If blessed, we return in the middle
of an argument, undone by the light
on our enemy's lip. Or while sharpening
a knife we cut ourselves and the trickle
of blood stains our list of grievances.
What if pain, the kind that opens a
fist, is really the tap of an angel
saving us from ourselves?

to embody or consume;
to be in kinship with everything larger
or to order and manage everything smaller.

We are asked, every day, to align or separate;
to coordinate our will with everything living
or to impose our will on everything we meet.

And not choosing is a choice. Acquiescence
is different from patience or surrender.

All this leaves us needing to know:
whether to better the song through practice
or to better ourselves through singing.

At the End of the Field

Side by side, two horses
work the same field for so long
that the plow that binds them
falls apart. For some time, they
drag the harness that has
tamed them.

One still feels the weight of the
plow, while the other knows
it is suddenly free.

They look at each other
as mirrors they fear. One keeps
plowing, even without a plow,
while the other, not knowing
where to go, leaves.

Exposed

Like a mountain
exposed for years,
the more worn I am,
the less there is
for climbers
to hold on to.

This doesn't mean
I'm untouchable,
just no longer
easy to cling to.

Like an inlet worn
by unceasing depths,
I can no longer decide
what belongs in or out.

This doesn't mean
I'm indecisive, just

flushed by experience
into a greater acceptance
of what life brings.

Like lilies set aflame,
I'm unable to hold
anything back.

INSIDE WHY

Violins are falling
from the sky. As they
tumble the wind releases
deep music. This is how
love sounds to itself. This
is what it's like to love
you. It's a music that
can't always be heard.
Instead, I run my hands
through your hair.

The Water Takes Many Forms

When people are at a loss, the guide ferries them over.
When one is (awake), one ferries oneself.
—*Hui-Neng*

Listen for guides, but use their wisdom as you
would a lamp to read your own heart. If someone dissuades you from your heart, they are not
a guide. A guide, like a ferryman, brings you
close to the water, will even help you cross,
but it's your own thirst that makes you cry
stop, wait—so you can drink.

When drinking of that water, it's clear:
the taste of birth we long to keep alive grows
inside everything. In the sheerness of the
water once it stops moving. In the surrender
of exhaustion that loosens every grip. In the
peace within our loneliness once we stop
gnawing at what might have been.

When drinking of that peace, it's clear:
doubt leads to humility, the way thirst makes
us drink. And pain drops into Oneness, the
way hunger makes us eat.

When finding a guide, listen, if you must, to
what they have to say, but look for the water
in their eyes and the wind that rims their
voice. Let your self be scoured back to the
beginning which is not behind us,
but about to crack open within us.

FALLING IN LOVE WITH THE WORLD

If we stay luminous in the whirl of existence,

who's to say we can't be stars for each other?

FALLING

Heavy drops, carrying more
than they can bear, fall from no-
where, bending leaves already
sagging, and one by one,
the leaves let go.

They drift to the earth,
each quiet as a master
juggler missing everything so
completely that he realizes
he is being juggled.

Surrender is like this.
Not giving up, but
missing and letting go.

BREAKING TRANCE

It's raining lightly and the sheep
are standing in the wet field, stopped
by beads of water from the sky on their
ears, their eyes, their mouths. They look
like statues breaking their trance. Alive
for the first time, they wonder, what is
this magical place where the very air
kisses you everywhere. Falling in
love with the world is like this.

Help me resist the urge
to dispute whether things
are true or false
which is like
arguing whether
it is day or night.

It is always
one or the other
somewhere in the world.

Together, we can penetrate
a higher truth which
like the sun is always
being conveyed.

FALLING
IN

I don't spend time with the broken
because I like pain, but because
I need to feel life
from inside its shell.

Everywhere I turn, I witness
such resilience breaking out of
ordinary people: the fourteen year
old who was burned saving her grand-
mother; the Black sergeant carrying his
white lieutenant out of live fire and how
they fell in the sand and cried in each
other's arms; and the one with no arms
who keeps asking what she can carry.

I'm watching a hummingbird now
work so hard, its wings seem not
to be moving at all. Is this what
happens when we love?

I'll tell you a secret. I ran a comb
through Grandma's hair minutes after
she died. She was still warm, her Spirit
on its way. I still have the comb. And
when in doubt or awe, I get by myself
and finger the spaces in
that comb.

How can I say this properly:
We can cheat death for a while
by feeding it things that are false.

And we can draw life out
by giving when we think
there's nothing left.

The Promise of
the Inner World

If you take away all a person knows,
you are left with the mouth of a fish
gulping water as fast as it can. If you
take away a person's coverings, you are
left with the naked freedom of a star.

If you take away all a person has done,
you are left with a soul eager to build.
And if you take away what a person has
saved, you are left with a life that
has to live now.

Stripped of too many thoughts, we
grow wise as a stone. Stripped of too
many accomplishments, we grow
possible like the sun. And stripped
of what we hoard, we grow immediate.

So taking away is not just about loss.
Like it or not, we are forced, again
and again, to the nakedness of freedom,
to the eagerness that wants to build its
way out of nothing, and to the poverty
of time that has to live now. If blessed,
we wake, one more time, gulping
our way into tomorrow.

What if love is the blood of God,
and only when carried in that river
are we touched by what is holy?

What if truth is carried in the
conversation of birds winging
through our silence, the way
quiet souls brave their way
through the lies we all agree to?

What if beauty is what's left
when the illusions are scoured away?
Air. Snow. Light on a fence that
kept out nothing anyway.

And running through it all,
the invisible river in which we
can barely speak except to say
thank you, I have been, I am,

like water or light, able
to help things grow.

WHAT SUSTAINS

The more I am hollowed
by the fire, the more my ribs
spread like the tree of life.

The more I am washed
by the tears of others, the more
my heart rounds like an ocean shell.

The more stories I tell
of how one picks up another,
the more my hands open
like scoops for grain.

To be what others drink,
to be what others stand on
to reach what they love—
we should be so lucky
to be worn to this.

FALLING
IN THE
WORLD

It's as if what is unbreakable—
the very pulse of life—waits for
everything else to be torn away,
and then in the bareness that
only silence and suffering and
great love can expose, it dares
to speak through us and to us.

It seems to say, if you want to last,
hold on to nothing. If you want
to know love, let in everything.
If you want to feel the presence
of everything, stop counting the
things that break along the way.

Putting
a child on a horse.

Hanging
silk to dry.

Watching
snow fill the crack
in a bridge.

Waiting
in the shadow of a bird.

Touching
the shoulder of the moon.

Wetting
the lips of one
who has given up.

Letting
the stone
in your heart crumble.

Placing
a flower over a blade.

Sitting
in a boat till
there is no ripple.

I was sipping coffee on the way to work,
the back road under a canopy of maples
turning orange. In the dip of woods, a small
doe gently leaping. I pulled over, for there
was no where else to go. She paused as if
she knew I was watching. A few orange
leaves fell around her like blessings no
one can seem to find. I sipped some
coffee, completely at peace, knowing
it wouldn't last. But that's alright.

We never know when we will blossom
into what we're supposed to be. It might
be early. It might be late. It might be after
thirty years of failing at a misguided way.
Or the very first time we dare to shed
our mental skin and touch the world.

They say, if real enough, some see God

at the moment of their death. But isn't
every fall and letting go a death? Isn't God
waiting right now in the chill between the
small doe's hoof and those fallen leaves?

G R A T I T U D E S

I began the long list of those I'm indebted to, but something in the nameless quality that this book rests on keeps deflecting such naming. Let me say plainly that gratitude and humility swell when thinking of those who've held me up, who've helped me endure the many ways I've been reduced and worn of my false-hoods through the years. I smile deeply when thinking of those who've opened me to the joy of simply being here. I would be less without these friendships. I love you all. I keep telling strang-ers: to be in the presence of those who can both share pain and celebrate just waking up, this is the answer to loneliness. Such friendship makes sharing pizza in a noisy pub and standing in silence as the old oak creaks all one could ask for. In truth, this process, of being worn to only what is raw and essential, never ends. It's as if a great bird lives inside the stone of our days and since no sculptor can free it, it has to wait for the elements to wear us down, till it is free to fly. Thank you for holding me up to the elements, and for freeing yourselves, and for the joy of these unexpected moments together.

NOTES

p. vii, epigraph: "I want nothing more..." George Seferis, from "An Old Man on the River Bank," in *George Seferis: Collected Poems*, translated by Edmund Keeley and Philip Sherrard. NJ: Princeton University Press, 1967, p. 291. © 1967 Princeton University Press, 1995 renewed PUP/1995 revised edition. Reprinted by permission of Princeton University Press.

p. 27, epigraph: "People say we're all seeking..." Joseph Campbell, from *The Power of Myth*, Joseph Campbell with Bill Moyers, edited by Betty Sue Flowers. NY: Doubleday, 1988, p. 5. Based on interviews with Bill Moyers in 1985-86.

pp. 40, 44: Earlier prose versions of these two poems originally appeared in my nonfiction book *Finding Inner Courage*: an excerpt from "Beginning Again" (appears here as "Behind the Thunder," p. 40) and an excerpt from "The Heart's Blossom" (appears here as "Made from Bone," p. 44). Excerpted from *Finding Inner Courage* © 2007 by Mark Nepo published by Red Wheel/ Weiser, LLC Newbury Port, MA and San Francisco, CA. www. redwheelweiser.com.

pp. 55, 123: Epigraphs to the two sections, "Till We Know Each Other" and "Falling in Love with the World," are the author's.

p. 84: The poem "The Throat of Dawn" appears in *Burning the Midnight Oil*, edited by Phil Cousineau, Viva Editions, 2013.

p. 87, epigraph: "To be poured into..." Chuang-Tzu, from *Chuang-Tzu: Mystic, Moralist, and Social Reformer*, translated by Herbert A. Giles. London: Quaritch, 1889, chapter 2.

p. 97, epigraph: "A fish cannot drown in water..." Mechthild, from *The Enlightened Heart*, edited by Stephen Mitchell. NY: Harper & Row, 1989, p. 64.

p. 121, epigraph: "When people are at a loss..." The quote in "The Water Takes Many Forms" is from *The Sutra of Hui-Neng: Grand Master of Zen*, translated by Thomas Cleary. Boston: Shambhala, 1998, p. 12.

p. 129: The poem "Restoring Confidence" first appeared in my book *Seven Thousand Ways to Listen*, Free Press, 2012, p. 103.

p. 143: The poem "Where Is God?" first appeared in the journal *Sufi*.

About the Author

MARK NEPO is a poet and philosopher who has taught in the fields of poetry and spirituality for forty years. A *New York Times* number one bestselling author, he has published fourteen books and recorded eight audio projects. Recent work includes: *Seven Thousand Ways to Listen* which won the 2012 Books for a Better Life Award, *Staying Awake* (2012), *Holding Nothing Back* (2012), *As Far As the Heart Can See* (2011), *Finding Inner Courage* (2011), and *Surviving Has Made Me Crazy* (2007), as well as audio books of *The Book of Awakening, Finding Inner Courage,* and *As Far As the Heart Can See* (2011). As a cancer survivor, Mark devotes his writing and teaching to the journey of inner transformation and the life of relationship.

Mark has appeared with Oprah Winfrey on her *Super Soul Sunday* program on OWN TV, and has been interviewed by Oprah as part of her SIRIUS XM Radio show, *Soul Series*. He has also been interviewed by Robin Roberts on *Good Morning America* about his *New York Times* bestseller *The Book of Awakening*. *The Exquisite Risk* was cited by *Spirituality & Practice* as one of the Best Spiritual Books of 2005, calling it "one of the best books we've ever read on what it takes to live an authentic life." Mark's collected essays appear in *Unlearning Back to God: Essays on Inwardness*. Other books of poetry include *Suite for the Living* (2004), *Inhabiting Wonder* (2004), *Acre of Light* (1994), *Fire Without Witness* (1988), and *God, the Maker of the Bed, and the Painter* (1988).

His work has been translated into more than twenty languages. In leading spiritual retreats, in working with healing and medical communities, and in his teaching as a poet, Mark's work is widely accessible and used by many. He continues to offer readings, lectures, and retreats. Please visit Mark at: www.MarkNepo.com, http://threeintentions.com, and www.simonspeakers.com/MarkNepo.

Author Photograph by Brian Bankston, www.brianbankston.com.

TO OUR READERS

Viva Editions publishes books that inform, enlighten, and entertain. We do our best to bring you, the reader, quality books that celebrate life, inspire the mind, revive the spirit, and enhance lives all around. Our authors are practical visionaries: people who offer deep wisdom in a hopeful and helpful manner. Viva was launched with an attitude of growth and we want to spread our joy and offer our support and advice where we can to help you live the Viva way: vivaciously!

We're grateful for all our readers and want to keep bringing you books for inspired living. We invite you to write to us with your comments and suggestions, and what you'd like to see more of. You can also sign up for our online newsletter to learn about new titles, author events, and special offers.

Viva Editions
2246 Sixth St.
Berkeley, CA 94710
www.vivaeditions.com
(800) 780-2279
Follow us on Twitter @vivaeditions
Friend/fan us on Facebook